The Mystery of Grace
in the Baptism of Our Children

Bart Garrett

Resource *Publications*

An imprint of *Wipf and Stock Publishers*
199 West 8th Avenue • Eugene OR 97401

THE MYSTERY OF GRACE IN THE BAPTISM OF OUR CHILDREN

Resource Publications
an imprint of Wipf & Stock Publishers

ISBN 10: 1-59752-848-X
ISBN 13: 978-1-59752-848-1

Manufactured in the U.S.A

Contents

Acknowledgments

Special thanks to my beautiful bride, Katie, and our three, precious little girls, each a blessing wrapped in a promise.

Thanks to my parents, hands that are steady, character that is deep, and a faith that seems unwavering—I learn from you both. From Corrie, a posture that questions the status quo—thanks for challenging me!

Thanks to Jonathan St. Clair, my partner in ministry and faithful friend. We share a brain, and he brings order to my abstraction. Thanks also to Scott Jones and Eric Youngblood. The three of us were inseparable in graduate school, and these two men are an integral part of who I am as a pastor.

Finally, it is rare for a day to go by when I do not stop and think: "What would Richard Pratt have to say about that?" Thanks Richard, for your voice that forever remains in the ear of your students.

Preface

Over the years I have talked to many well meaning, sincere couples who grapple with the Christian doctrine of infant baptism. "Jesus was baptized as an adult." "The New Testament never really talks about baptizing babies, so why should we do it now?" "It just will not be as meaningful when she is a little baby." "The Bible says, 'Repent, believe and then get baptized.' How can little babies demonstrate repentance and faith?" "I want him to appreciate Christ and come to trust in Him for salvation; then baptism will actually mean something to him." "Jesus came up out of the Jordan River. You mean to tell me that just sprinkling a couple of drops on my baby's head does the trick?"

This booklet is an attempt to deal with those sincere, heart-felt questions in a pastoral way. It is not an attempt to defend my case, prove my point, or eviscerate those who believe differently. As a pastor, one of my greatest privileges is to hold a precious, little child in my arms, pray for her, pray for her parents, and counsel our congregation towards recognizing that, in our very midst, this little one has the opportunity to learn the ways of our Savior. I then have the blessing of baptizing her. I hope this booklet will be useful in helping parents understand more fully the wonderful gift and privilege of baptism that God has given to the children of believers.

Chapter 1 Pastoral Counsel

Wisdom is the God-given ability to discern which issues are most and least significant, which issues are most and least clear. Wisdom helps us distinguish between a mere preference, which is to be held more loosely, and a conviction, which should be held more tightly. Many biblical scholars have demonstrated quite adequately that baptism should be limited to people who have made a profession of faith in Christ and that the practice should not include their children. Other scholars have demonstrated quite adequately that baptism should be extended to those who have professed faith in Christ *and* to their children. Years ago, as a graduate student, I wrestled with great intensity over this issue. For months, on my bedside table was a stack of about twelve books, precariously positioned, suspended over the pillow on which I slept. Typically, on the subject of baptism, I held to the convictions of the author of the book that sat upon the top of the stack. Needless to say, my opinions on the matter changed every other week.

As people get older they become *more* certain of *fewer* things. We begin to understand that there is really a lot that we do not know; yet what we have come to know we hold with even greater fervor and passion than we once did. What are the *few* things that I am *most* certain about? Christ died. Christ has risen. Christ will come again. And these three are clear enough in the Scriptures, which we believe speak to us with authority because they come from God. Finally, my only comfort in both life and death is that I am utterly dependent on Jesus for salvation, and I trust that he will come through brilliantly in the end, completing the work of refining someone as selfish and insecure as I am.

Please recognize that baptism is a very important issue, but I do not think it is an essential one. If it were, then while on the cross, Jesus would not have refused the wine-soaked sponge, but would have accepted it in order to sprinkle some on the thief that had just trusted in him for salvation. Yet, instead, with no formal baptismal rite, Jesus responded: "Today, you will be with me in paradise." It is important that sincere parents come to resolution on this issue. Yet, I am not so sure that their resolution will arise from calculated study and an effort to gather and collect all of the data. There is simply too much to consider on both sides of this issue. Rather, resolution will hopefully come with a sincere submission to the authority of the pastor that serves your respective church.

As a pastor, I long for the day when parishioners will again exercise confidence and trust in their church leadership. With the scandal of sexual and financial impropriety dotting the clerical landscape, I realize that this is a grandiose request. Yet, the Bible is full of admonitions that beckon believers to submit to the authority of their pastors and shepherds. I recognize that the term, "authority," today is fraught with negative connotation, yet it is important to recognize that all of us submit to authority, whether that authority be *the authority of autonomy* or whether is be *the authority of a particular belief system or ideology.* The chief reason that I pastor a church that belongs to a larger denomination is this one: I want to shepherd our people while in submission to many leaders who are more seasoned, and thus, more wise, than I am. I need the accountability. Our church needs the accountability. In a society where large corporations are granted privileges and incentives permitting them the power to make unwise decisions unilaterally, it is important to me that the church remains in submission to the accountability of a larger entity like a denomination.

Likewise, there are many perplexing issues like baptism that create opportunity for sincere church members to submit their confusion and uncertainty to the counsel of the pastoral leadership. On these important, yet non-essential issues, allow the leadership to shape policy—policy that has been wrestled through with a certain degree of theological skill and expertise. Then, be willing to embrace the outcomes. The Bible teaches that teachers will be held to a higher standard of accountability, thus, take the pressure off of your own shoulders and let us bear it for you. Baptism is a very important issue. It is not an essential issue.[1] Deference to your leadership and the present community in which you worship is perhaps more pleasing to God than your own personal opinions and premonitions about baptism itself.[2]

---

[1] See James 3:1.

[2] I choose to highlight deference to one's authority, not because it is primary, but because, today in America, it is largely treated as ancillary. Difficult decisions like these are best made from various sources of input, from our present community, from its leadership, and from our personal convictions as they are informed by the Scriptures.

Chapter 2 An Important Qualification

BAPTISM IS not necessary for salvation, nor does it procure it. Sadly, throughout history, blood has been spilled over this issue. The language of the Bible is gripping and even provocative,[3] and one unfortunate result is that erroneous conclusions about baptism have been drawn. Baptism symbolizes a great deal. The powerful descriptions of baptism in the Bible push people to look beyond *baptism as symbol* to find *baptism as salvation.* One passage often cited by those who see baptism as a saving act:

> ". . . And this water symbolizes *baptism* that now saves you also—not the removal of dirt from the body but the pledge of a good conscience toward God. It saves you by the resurrection of Jesus Christ." (1 Peter 3:21)

I must admit, I am often a little perplexed when people point to this verse as a "proof-text" for baptism's power to save us. In fact, it says explicitly in this verse that baptism, in this context, does not refer to the *ritual*, the physical act of washing with water, but to the *promise*, the spiritual reality that salvation has been committed to us through the Resurrection of Jesus.

Sincere Christians are in agreement on this essential issue: the "Good News" of the Gospel is that our salvation is premised on God's grace and mercy and not our own desire or effort.[4] We agree that symbol, rite, and human observance do not merit salvation, only God's grace does! Baptism, like any other spiritual practice or observance, is done not to *earn* God's favor, but rather, to *respond* to it.

---

[3] See Galatians 3:27.

[4] See Titus 3:5.

Chapter 3 Mode and Meaning

Sometimes pastors from other denominations voice their concerns to me about our practice of infant baptism, and their concerns can be lumped into two categories: (1) the mode of infant baptism, and (2) the meaning of infant baptism. The *mode* refers primarily to how much water is used in the application of baptism. Is water sprinkled over the one receiving the baptism? Or, is it poured? Is the person dipped in water or completely immersed under the water? This booklet will only address the *meaning* of baptism simply because, in my opinion, the *mode* of baptism is of little or no consequence. If you agree with me on this point, then feel free to skip over this section, but for those who might not, it is appropriate to offer my rationale, albeit a brief one.

When baptism is mentioned in the New Testament it often involves the subject "going down into the water" (Acts 8:38)[5] and "coming up out of the water" (Matthew 3:16). It is only natural that many sincere people assume that this was an act of immersion, and then think that this particular action is normative for the rite of baptism today. [6] After all, if baptism symbolizes being buried with Jesus in death and then raised with him to newness of life,[7] then it is only right to assume that immersing someone all the way under the water and then bringing them up again paints the clearest picture.[8] Yet, by contrast, in

---

[5] It might also be worth noting that when the Ethiopian eunuch asked Philip to baptize him, he had just heard the Gospel as presented in Isaiah 52 and 53, a passage that deals with, ironically (or perhaps providentially), the "sprinkling" ministry of the Lord.

[6] Please note that these descriptions do not necessarily imply that people were immersed completely under the water. It is just as likely that people stepped into the water and then had the water poured over their heads. This is not an academic paper, but suffice it to say here, the semantic range of the Greek prepositions in the text will certainly allow, and might even imply, that this is the case.

[7] See Romans 6:4.

[8] Of course, in those days, many people were buried laterally in tombs rather than under the earth, and so, perhaps the most appropriate symbolic mode of baptism would be to push some-

the proper observance of the sacrificial system as outlined in the Old Testament, Israelites were usually identified with the atoning sacrifice that they carried into the Temple by having the blood of the animal sprinkled upon them[9] or poured over the mercy seat of the Ark of the Covenant; they were never completely submerged in blood (thank goodness).

The Greek word for baptism (*baptizo*) has a much broader range of meaning (semantic range) than the tightly defined "to immerse." Now, most certainly, "to immerse" is a valid translation, but so is "to wash," "to dip," "to sprinkle," "to suffuse," or "to pour." The simple point is that what was meant by the term, *baptizo*, is not precisely clear to us today. Perhaps people were immersed completely, or perhaps they waded out into the water and then had the water sprinkled or poured over their heads. We are not sure. In fact, the only baptism in the New Testament that mentions the *type* of mode explicitly is the Baptism of the Holy Spirit in which the Spirit is *poured over* the church at Pentecost.[10]

---

one under a large waterfall and then pull them out of it (laterally as to demonstrate walking out of the tomb). But we will not discuss these matters here.

[9] See Exodus 24:8.

[10] See Joel 2; Acts 2.

Chapter 4 The Meaning of Baptism

The Context Of Understanding

LET'S SAY that I approached you in the early afternoon of a crisp, fall day in the park and asked, "Why is the sky blue?" You might respond, "It has much to do with refracted and reflected light, how our retina is processing a flurry of colors emanating from the light of the sun, but being filtered through various gases and entities in our atmosphere." Or you could say, "Evil aliens have covered our earth in a blue soup, prohibiting us from seeing their cadre of spaceships that are preparing to descend upon our planet in order to mount an attack."[11] Your answer is dependent upon your *context of understanding.*[12] Your understanding of the sky's "blueness" is dependent upon your frame of reference. Likewise, an understanding of baptism is dependent upon a particular frame of reference (*context of understanding*), and an important task of biblical interpretation is to propose what that particular *context of understanding* might have been for the people who were living during the time that the Bible was written.

An astute reader of the Bible would acknowledge that the *context of understanding* for the Israelite was the administration of a Covenant between God and Creation. This covenant ordered the relationship. The communication, the expectations, the promises, the outcomes (whether they be blessings or curses), etc. of that relationship were mediated through this covenant. There are specific instances in Scripture where this "covenant conversation" moves to the fore. It is during these conversations where the covenant gets nuanced and adjusted

[11] This is a variation of an illustration used in John Stackhouse' book, *Humble Apologetics* (Oxford University Press, 2002).

[12] And might I add, that if your *context of understanding* is the latter rather than the former, then, by all means, please allow me to recommend a good therapist.

while still retaining certain distinguishing attributes that enable it to maintain its unique place as the covenant between God and his people.

The first covenant conversation is between God and Adam and serves as a promise of God's provision and protection for all humanity. This provision is contingent upon the corresponding faithfulness of humanity. Upon the destruction brought on by the flood, God engages in a second covenant conversation, this time with Noah, asserting his promise never again to destroy the earth with water, coupled with the corresponding faithfulness of humanity. Thirdly, God approaches Abraham, and their conversation holds the promise that, from Abraham, God will raise up a mighty people that he will call to fulfill his purposes, granting them also the land of promise in exchange for their faithfulness. Fourthly, Moses and God enter into covenant conversation concerning the specific laws that would shape and mold the people of God. Once the nation of Israel is established, God extends his covenant through King David, asserting that the Messiah will emerge from David's royal, ancestral line. And finally, the ultimate covenant conversation is between Father and Son, as Jesus, by his once-and-for-all sacrifice, renews and secures a covenant relationship between God and creation, a relationship that had become fractured, but through Christ is being "filled up again"[13] with great meaning.

With each and every covenant conversation comes greater clarity and meaning with respect to this relationship shared between God and his people. And as each covenant conversation puts paint on the canvas, we notice that the covenantal blessings are contingent upon our faithfulness. The condition for God's blessing is the faithfulness of His people. Unfaithfulness will be punished as the curses of the covenant fall upon the people. All of us break under the weight of this reality, for who can remain faithful to these obligations? Yet, our hope is in Jesus, who becomes broken for us, and by his stripes we are healed,[14] by his obedience we are saved and the covenant conversation ensues unhindered, the covenant unbroken.

It is important to view the New Testament through these lenses, through this *context of understanding*. For a Jewish person living in the first century (the time of Jesus), relationship with God would be understood most fully in the context of the Covenant. This notion of Covenant was not a concept that

[13] *Fulfilled* in Scripture often means: "Filling-filling; a more than filling."

[14] See Isaiah 53.

was made up by God, divorced from any sort of historical relevance or parallel. Rather, in those times, covenant was the understood administration of the relationship between a King and his subjects, creating a *context of understanding* that helped the Jews understand these relational dynamics with greater clarity and precision. The covenant relationship seen as such often involved particular *symbols of meaning* and was forged between *particular kinds of people.* Let us spend a little time looking at both of these.

The Symbols Of The Covenant

Relationships are forged with signs, symbols, seals, and tokens of affection. Most happily married couples have a favorite, romantic place, preserve a certain love letter, pull out footage from the wedding ceremony from time to time, celebrate a day of anniversary, cherish an engagement ring and wedding band, and relish in a special gift given on a special occasion. Our relationship with God is no different. Signs, symbols, seals, and tokens of affections are essential to our relationship with God—it would not be complete without them.

Today, the covenant relationship that the church enjoys with God is undergirded by two important symbols that we call sacraments (from the Latin *sacramentum,* meaning "mystery"). They are Baptism and Holy Communion.[15] The Scriptures paint a picture of baptism as a rite of initiation into the community or covenant relationship (much like the wedding ring), and portray Holy Communion as an ongoing rite of continuation (much like, perhaps, the celebration of the wedding anniversary—a celebration that cherishes what has happened in the past, applauds the intimacy of the present, and hopes for abundant joy in the future).

In the marital relationship, tokens of affection come with a treasured story, and in a similar way, the covenant signs and seals did not appear *ex nihilo,* but rather, emerged from a rich history and, more poignantly, a direct initiative from God. Most Christians are aware of the origination of Holy Communion.[16] Jesus gathered the disciples in an upper room during the Passover Feast (the feast memorializing the deliverance of the people of God from their slavery in

[15] The Roman Catholic Church recognizes seven sacraments. Much is written on the broader Catholic definition for "sacrament," and the more specific, Protestant definition, but this is beyond the scope of this booklet.

[16] Also called Eucharist and/or the Lord's Supper.

Egypt), and using some of the symbols from the feast itself (the Seder Meal), initiated a supper involving bread and wine, his body and blood, as a remembrance for each of us, signifying who he is and what he came to do.

But from where did the sign and seal (the symbol) of baptism originate? The first baptism we find in the New Testament is the baptism of Jesus by John the Baptist.[17] Was this a new symbol that John the Baptizer concocted while a lonely wanderer in the wilderness? Its practice certainly added a little pizzazz to his otherwise common name.

We will address that question, but before we do, hold on to it for a minute, and let us quickly explore another ritual (another sign and seal) that we find in the New Testament: the rite of circumcision. We do not have to wait (as if we *were* waiting) very long to have circumcision uncovered for us in the New Testament. Jesus was circumcised and presented at the Temple on the eighth day, as was customary for Jewish, baby boys.[18] And in the pages that follow, there are discussions on the meaning and implication of circumcision. These passages are found all over the New Testament. In fact, the Apostle Paul talks more about circumcision than he does anything else. Because its presence is ubiquitous, it is evident that this rite was of utmost importance to the people of God. It originated with Abraham.[19] God commanded Abraham to circumcise himself (at 90 years old!) and every male in his house. This was to be, God said, a "sign of the covenant," representing the "cutting away" of man's unfaithfulness in order to demonstrate faithful obedience to God. In other words, circumcision became *the outward sign of an inner faith.*[20]

Okay, I want you to keep circumcision on your brain for a few minutes (sorry I'm making you do that), but I want to get back to our question with regards to baptism: Where did it come from? Did John create the practice of baptism or was he extending the meaning of a ritual that was already recognizable to the people of God? History teaches the latter. John's baptism in the dessert was a baptism of repentance. It was not something that was entirely new. The cleansing rites for people entering the Temple in the Old Testament were quite elaborate. These ritual cleansings were in essence, baptisms. They were the

[17] See Mark 1; Luke 3; Matthew 3.

[18] See Luke 2.

[19] See Genesis 17.

[20] Romans 4:11 makes this meaning very clear: "He received the sign of circumcision, a seal of the righteousness that he had by faith while he was still uncircumcised."

symbolic, *outward expression of an inner purity.*[21] It was *the outward sign of an inner faith.* Sound familiar?

It is not hard to see a parallel meaning emerge between the sign of circumcision and the sign of baptism. *Both were outward signifiers of an inner purity.* In the Intertestamental Period (the 400 years between the Old and New Testaments), the Jews used baptism to cleanse Gentile converts, both male and female, as well as corrupted Jews. Additionally, the males were circumcised, often during the baptismal ritual itself. These two signs (circumcision and baptism) were coupled together into one particular rite of passage, and this is quite significant as we address our contemporary *context of understanding.*

Circumcision and Baptism were outward, physical signs demonstrating inward, spiritual realities. In the New Testament, when the Gospel first went forth, it went to the Jews, those who were already circumcised. Thus, only baptism was added as a sign of faith. Yet, as the Gospel spread, Gentiles were being converted, and the question arose, "We are baptizing, but should we circumcise these new converts as well?" This is the question that prompted the leaders of the church to convene the Jerusalem Council.[22] At that council, the pillars of the church spoke: "Because the ingathering of Gentiles into our fold fulfills the Old Testament, it is our calling to make their initiation as easy on them as possible."[23] In their application, the knife of circumcision, as it was to be applied to the Gentile converts, was dropped. Thus, we have a definitive point in history where baptism replaces circumcision. Baptism, once a dual sign (with circumcision) signifying a single rite of passage for the Jews, became the sole sign for the Gentiles, and this sign identified them as a part of the covenant people.[24]

---

[21] A common question: Why did Jesus need to be baptized? This is, of course, well beyond the scope of this booklet, but suffice it to say here in this footnote, that this is the very same question that John asked of Jesus (Matthew 3) to which Jesus replied, "It must be so now to fulfill all righteousness." We might understand this quote as follows: "To bring about God's unfolding will in place and time." In other words, this baptism set John apart as the new Elijah, the messenger in the desert, and set Jesus apart as, "the One who was to come." This act fulfilled prophecy and identified Jesus as the true Israelite who would keep the whole of the Law. This cleansing act was not for his sins, but for our own.

[22] See Acts 15 on the Jerusalem Council.

[23] My paraphrase of Acts 15:9.

[24] See Richard Pratt's "Why Do We Baptize Our Children?" His unfolding of the history of these two signs of covenant initiation is excellent and helpful.

Yet, to some people, this logical, historical progression—the rite of passage including both baptism and circumcision, with circumcision later being eclipsed—seems circumspect, seemingly lacking explicit biblical reference. "I want to see the passage of Scripture that explicitly references baptism as the natural replacement of circumcision," one might remark. I have often said in response, "Well, you will not find said passage, for the argument is usually inferred, as Jews would have clearly understood this natural progression in their respective context." However, the more I read Colossians 2:11,12 in light of the appropriate, Jewish *context of understanding*, the more I am beginning to recognize it as an explicit reference to baptism as the replacement to circumcision:

> "In him you were also circumcised, in the putting off of the sinful nature, not with a circumcision done by the hands of men but with the circumcision done by Christ, having been buried with him in baptism and raised with him through your faith in the power of God, who raised him from the dead."

Paul is suggesting that Christ's circumcision is not a physical circumcision ("done by the hands of men"), but rather, it is a spiritual circumcision, one wrought through the sign and seal of baptism, the sign received by the people of God, as *explicitly* mentioned in this passage.

Perhaps you are beginning to understand, generally speaking, the relationship between the covenant and the signs, and more specifically, the relationship between the sign of circumcision and the sign of baptism as each applied to the Jew and the Gentile, at least those who were constituted as the people of God. But, this begs the question: "Who are the people of God?" You might be wondering, "Why baptize babies? If the sign is indeed an outward symbol of an inward reality, then why baptize a baby? They do not and cannot exercise faith.[25] It doesn't make much sense!" Perhaps it will make more sense when we look at one last entity, the people of God, the people of the covenant.

[25] While not the point of the discussion, one could argue that it is presumptuous of us know-it-all-adults to pretend to know what babies can and cannot do. Babies demonstrate a love *for* their parents and a trust *in* their parents. Could they not also, possibly, exercise similar faith in God?

The People of the Covenant

When God engages in covenant conversation with his people in the Old Testament, we clearly see that it his intention to include both *adults and their children*. In fact, the gracious covenant extended beyond the family to the household as well, to the "aliens and strangers within the gates."[26] In conversation with Adam,[27] Noah,[28] Abraham,[29] Moses,[30] and David,[31] children are *always* mentioned as those who also participate in the covenant. More specifically, we see with Abraham,[32] that the sign of circumcision was to be applied not only to himself ("one who believed"), but also to each and every male in his household. This included the young boy, Ishmael, and Isaac as well, the son who was yet to be born, and thus, certainly could not yet exercise personal faith.

It is very important for us to wrestle with the meaning and application of baptism today in light of this *context of understanding*. For the first-century Jew, there would be no need to mention explicitly the inclusion of children in God's covenant and in the signs of that covenant, for this would be understood. They would infer that this New Covenant in Jesus would certainly be more inclusive, not less inclusive than the old one. After all, circumcision was a male-only rite, while baptism was to be applied to both men and women. Would the new covenant sign of baptism be applied to both males and females (an inclusive push towards equality), yet not to both adults and children (an exclusionary push towards inequality)? "I think not," they would argue.

Furthermore, while there is no need to mention the inclusion of children explicitly due to the implicit inference made by first century Jews, it seems that the New Testament still intends to do so. As Peter preaches the Gospel of

---

[26] Many secularists point to the violence and hegemony found in the Old Testament as proof that the Bible is both historically primitive and socially regressive. Yet, the Israelites were actually less violent and more inclusive than most, if not all, other ancient Near Eastern peoples. Our God is one who tends to work through secondary causes and means, which include the imperfections and even the sins of people, in order to accomplish his ultimate plans and purposes.

[27] See Genesis 2; 3.

[28] See Genesis 9.

[29] See Genesis 12; 15; 17.

[30] See Exodus 20.

[31] See Psalm 89; 132.

[32] See Genesis 17.

the New Covenant at Pentecost, his rising crescendo is a pronouncement of these words: "Repent and be baptized, every one of you, in the name of Jesus Christ for the forgiveness of your sins. And you will receive the gift of the Holy Spirit. The promise is for you and your children and for all who are far off —for all whom the Lord our God will call."[33] Peter's announcement leverages "dusted-off," covenantal language, which stems straight from the words of the Old Testament.[34] In the ears of the Jewish people, the words would ring in a way that proffered an understanding of the covenant as more *inclusive* than ever before; it was a covenant for men and women, adults and children, Jews and Gentiles alike.

[33] See Acts 2:38-39.

[34] See Genesis 50:21; Leviticus 10:14-15; Deuteronomy 4:40; Deuteronomy 12:25,28; Deuteronomy 30:2,19; Psalm 115:14; Isaiah 49:25.

Chapter 5 The True Question Behind the Discussion

As you read, there is still one question that might remain: "What then, is *new* about the New Covenant?" The answer to this question will frame your decision to either baptize your children as infants or to wait until they have made a profession of faith. Jeremiah prophesied that God was to establish a New Covenant with his people; a covenant (1) that could not be broken with a people, of which, (2) every single one of them would exercise personal faith in him.[35] Later, Jesus announces that the Kingdom of God has come to earth, his spilled blood the installation of this New Covenant.[36] Still later, the letter to the Hebrews would announce that the New Covenant has rendered the Old Covenant obsolete, a strong word that we cannot simply "shirk" away, as if it is of no consequence. What is going on behind the scenes? It seems that the *newness* of the New Covenant is in fact *radical newness*, and thus, what should we make of it?

Because of this stark *newness* initiated by the New Covenant, some people have misread the emphasis on newness as the indication that: (1) The Old Covenant was conditional (dependant on the people's obedience), while the New Covenant is unconditional (doesn't depend on our obedience). (2) The Old Covenant included people that didn't exercise faith (foreigners and children) while the New Covenant is specifically made between those who profess faith *in their hearts* (allusion to the words of Jeremiah 31). (3) The Old Covenant is merely physical, while the New Covenant is wholly spiritual. The first two points hold the most weight with regard to this discussion, and are also interrelated, so I will address them first and will also address them in tandem. The third is ancillary and I will deal with it last.

---

[35] See Jeremiah 31:34: "They will all know me."

[36] See Mark 1:15 as a reference to the Kingdom of God. See Luke 22:20 as a reference to the New Covenant.

(1) *The Old Covenant was conditional (dependant on the people's obedience), while the New Covenant is unconditional (doesn't depend on our obedience).*

(2) *The Old Covenant included people that didn't exercise faith (foreigners and children) while the New Covenant is specifically made between those who exercise faith in their hearts (allusion to Jeremiah 31), thus why would we baptize (initiate) babies into a covenant relationship that is only to be forged with believers?*

We have addressed the conditionality of the covenant in the chapter on the *context of understanding,* yet, it is prudent to touch on it again here. It would be compelling to envision that what garners the New Covenant's *new-ness,* is its "unconditionality," meaning that while the Old Covenant was replete with conditions of obedience, the New Covenant is not, and thus, can never be broken. Yet, this is simply not the case. The very same verses that seem to speak of people losing their salvation, the verses that often wreak havoc on people's assurance of faith (Hebrews 6 and 10 for starters), are the passages that demonstrate, in fact, that the New Covenant contains conditions (covenant loyalty/faithfulness), and when those conditions are not met, the covenant is broken. More poignantly, because the New Covenant is a conditional covenant, the cross of Christ retains a greater worth. Jesus himself had to die in order to receive the covenant curses that we deserved (thus, the condition of the covenant was met), and to grant us finally, the covenant blessings that his death and resurrection procured. And so, salvation *cannot* be lost, but many who are not saved *can* fall out of the covenant by their unfaithfulness, demonstrating that perhaps we are looking at the *newness* of the New Covenant inappropriately. The New Covenant rightly includes both those who are saved and those who are not.

Let me state this very clearly: Am I saying that the New Covenant is the framework for the relationship between God and his people, and that some of these people are not actually *saved* as we understand the regeneration of their heart, but will actually one day fall under the curses of the New Covenant? Yes, that is exactly what I am saying. And this is not merely what *I* am saying, it is what the author of Hebrews is saying: "How much more severely do you think a man deserves to be punished who has trampled the Son of God under foot, who has treated as an unholy thing the blood of the covenant that *sanctified* him, and who has insulted the Spirit of grace?"[37] This passage in Hebrews is not talking about someone who has found salvation and then loses it, for that is impossible.[38] Instead, this passage, is using the word, *sanctified,* in the sense of "setting someone apart." [39] It does not mean setting them apart *for salvation,* but rather, setting them apart *in the context of covenant,* setting them out of the world and into the covenant.

"But, I just don't understand? Jeremiah seems to speak about the New Covenant as a relationship with God where no one will need to read the law from tablets of stone, because it will be ingrained upon our hearts? The book of Hebrews repeats this very same language.[40] I just don't get it? It seems to say that people in the New Covenant are only those who are saved?" This line of thinking is only partially accurate. In other words, while this is true of the New Covenant *ultimately*, it is not true *immediately*. This understanding fails to take into consideration what the church has spent two millennia grappling with in reference to the New Covenant. Its administration was only *initiated* by the coming of Christ (his death and resurrection); it was *not* brought to completion. Its fulfillment will happen only when Christ returns to sit on the throne as the ultimate judge over creation. At that time Jeremiah's New Covenant will be fully realized.[41]

The scope of the New Testament (its narratives, its poetry, its letters, its apocalyptic literature) wrestles with the tension that the New Covenant is coming in stages, and is not administered all at once. Jesus came. But then he left, to one-day come again. Thus, we will one day enjoy a reality where no one will need to go to his or her neighbor and exclaim, "Know the Lord," (Jeremiah 31), but that reality is not yet *this* day. It is only when Jesus will come back to consummate the work that he began. In practice, this is why we still have preachers, and why we still carry Bibles. Neighbors need to know the Lord so they must be taught (they must be taught despite what Jeremiah 31 says about the New

---

37 See Hebrews 10:29.

38 See passages like Philippians 1:6; I John 5:14; Ephesians 1:13-14; John 10:28.

39 Another passage where this is the case is I Corinthians 7:14.

40 See Hebrews 8.

41 For us, judgment often carries very negative connotations. Yet, the more pervasive understanding of judgment in Scripture is that it involves the establishment of a peaceful equality, where the marginalized and disadvantaged are lifted up and exalted. May we anticipate judgment with great sobriety, but also with great hope, as its pronouncement will "make all things right and new."

Covenant). We still do not have the Law of the Lord engraved upon our hearts so we must carry Bibles (again contrast Jeremiah 31). Hence, Jesus told parables such as that of the wheat and the tares,[42]reminding us that in his covenant community, there are some that know him, and others who do not, and the latter will be sifted upon the end of the age.[43]

(3) The Old Covenant was merely physical, while the New Covenant is wholly spiritual.[44]

This particular (and truncated) understanding of the Old and New Covenant is used, primarily, to bolster the distinctions between the kinds of people that are in the Old and the New Covenant and their practices. For instance, the Old Covenant is said to be administered through *physical* sacrifice, yet in the New Covenant, what is needed is *spiritual* sacrifice (Hebrews 13:15). On the surface this seems compelling, yet when we look more closely we see that spiritual sacrifice is offered in the Old Covenant (Psalm 51:17), and physical sacrifice is offered in the New Covenant ("sharing" in Hebrews 13:16).

In summary, how then is the New Covenant, *new*? It is not *new* in the sense that it is now unconditional, for as we have seen, it was imperative that Christ meet its conditions and we persevere in faithfulness. It is not *new* in the sense that it only contains believers, for as we have seen, Jesus himself mentions that this is not the case (the teaching on the wheat and the tares), and the author of Hebrews addresses similar subject matter. It is not *new* in the sense that it is solely spiritual rather than physical, for, as we have seen, both the Old and the New administration of the covenant retain aspects that are both physical and

[42] See Matthew 13.

[43] Here is a helpful metaphor for our understanding of Old Testament prophecy as it relates to the coming of the Messiah and the ushering in of the New Covenant: The prophets of old looked upon the horizon and as they viewed the distant, mountain range, they saw the mountain of New Testament fulfillment, which would one day bring resolution to their Old Testament promises. Yet, as they journeyed towards this particular topography, they began to comprehend with greater clarity, and by the day of Jesus, understood that the mountain of fulfillment was in fact, two mountains. One mountain sprung into view when Jesus came (the Inauguration of the Kingdom); the other will be recognized when Jesus comes back (the Consummation of the Kingdom). In the meantime, we live in the valley between the two, namely, the Valley of Continuation, in which, the church toils to bring the final mountain into lucid view. (Special thanks to Richard Pratt for popularizing this language).

[44] Wayne Grudem has codified this belief in his "Systematic Theology." It should not go without saying that I humbly disagree with him on this point, as he is a reputable scholar.

spiritual. It *is new* in that it is has been "re-newed" by Christ. What was broken and in disrepair, became reshaped and remade in order to be *renewed.* And this renewal is indeed radically significant (radical enough to render language like *obsolete* useful; see Hebrews 8) because the covenant keeper is Jesus, not a mere human, but God himself. He will indeed remain faithful and will be true to both his word and his actions, and these will bring about the ultimate fulfillment of the covenant.

Chapter 6 Will You Please Summarize?

In deference to mommies and daddies who spend most of their leisure time sucking up mashed Cheerios™ and raisins with a vacuum from under the seats of the minivan, in *short*, what does all of this mean for the baptism of children? Consider this a summary for the harried, stressed-out, exhausted parent, the one who is merely trying to get to church with the diaper bag, the wipes, and the formula, while wearing both shoes, and having successfully changed into something a little more presentable than PJ's. Why is it my hope that you, in deference to your pastoral leadership, which seeks to lead in a posture of submission and humility, will choose to baptize your children? Below is my "parents' cheat-sheet" answer to that question.

- You would recognize that our relationship with God is ordered by a covenant, and this covenant is replete with signs and symbols, these being spiritual tokens of affection and commitment to God, much like those that you would find in the marital relationship.
- You would recognize that the sign of *initiation* into this covenant relationship is the sign of baptism, and it functions much like an engagement ring; it is the outward sign of an inner commitment (faith).
- You would recognize that the rite of baptism was not a New Testament invention, but was originally coupled with the rite of circumcision, and both signified outwardly this inner commitment (faith).
- You would recognize that circumcision was initially applied to an adult believer (Abraham) and his children. For the adult it was an outward sign of an inner reality, and for the child, it would call the child towards one day making this inner commitment (faith).

- You would recognize that baptism naturally replaced circumcision as the Gospel went forth to the Gentiles. People living in those times would have inferred that baptism would most certainly retain the similar principles of circumcision, yet would be even more inclusive. While circumcision was for the head of the household (in those days, the father), and for his infant, male-children, baptism would be even more inclusive, not less. Baptism would be for the male and female, the Jew and Gentile, the adult and child alike.

- You would recognize that including your child in the sacrament of baptism does not violate the *newness* of the New Covenant, because the newness of the New Covenant is not premised upon it's being merely for believing adults. Rather, its newness is centered upon the completed, once-and-for-all work of Christ, a work that renders our meager ability to be faithful, obsolete.

- You would recognize that you would not baptize your child because you think that this act of baptism saves your child. God saves us by his grace, not by our ritual performance. In this sense, baptism is not primarily about doing our part, but about God's promise. As surely as the water washes a baby's head, we can earnestly expect that God will invade that baby's heart with the cleansing and renewing Holy Spirit.

- Instead, baptize your child because you recognize that it demonstrates symbolically, union with Christ, the cleansing of sin, the renewal by the Spirit, and in all of this, is a *means of God's grace.*

We have not dealt specifically with this concept of the *means of grace*, and so, let us address it in conclusion.[45] Too often, our westernized understanding

[45] This booklet has not dealt with the historical arguments for infant baptism (R.C. Sproul offers much insight here in a series of tapes from the 1999 Ligonier Conference in which he debates the issue with Alistair Begg). Suffice it to say here in this footnote, until the reformation, infant baptism was the normal practice. The earliest references to infant baptism are found in the middle of the third century, credited to Origen, Tertullian, and Iranaeus. Origen remarks, "Infant baptism was the universal custom of the church rooted and grounded in the apostolic tradition." Many Baptists appeal to this history and say, "Well, why are there no earlier references? Why don't we hear of infant baptism until the middle of the third century? This should demonstrate that perhaps a seed of confusion has crept into the church late in the game."

However, consider the history behind the history. Let us suppose that for 250 years after Christ,

of faith is that of a rugged, pioneering, radically individualistic faith. Faith is between you and God. It has little to do with other people.[46] Yet, the Bible, as it describes moving towards maturity, often couches its methodology in the context of community, and more specifically, in the church community. It is in the church community where God's means of grace—the teaching of His word, the offering of his sacraments (Holy Communion and Baptism), and prayer—are administered to God's people. These means do not procure our salvation, but be assured, they most certainly are the normal means of bringing it about.

Understanding baptism as a *means of grace* should help us with this booklet's thesis-question: Why should I baptize my infant? You should baptize your child because God specifies that baptism is one of the usual means that God uses to dispense his grace. Think about it much like you would a backyard garden. When you construct the garden, the expert you consult will instruct you: "Remember, there are five things that you should do to help your garden grow. It must get adequate sunlight, appropriate rainfall, and intentional fertilization. The holes that you dig in order to plant the seeds should be of suitable depth,

---

the church only practiced believer's baptism, and then, all of a sudden, the church switched its methodology, and infant baptism became as Origen says, ". . . the universal custom." History is full of treatise after treatise on theological debates concerning the Trinity, the deity of Christ, the means of salvation, etc, etc. Certainly someone would raise a red flag on this issue and protest this new, spurious doctrine. Yet we cannot find one document that does so. Logic tells us that there wasn't any debate because everyone understood that it was the universal practice to place the sign of the New Covenant upon the head of both the parent and the child. R.C. Sproul remarks, "It did not become an issue until the church corrupted infant baptism in the same way Israel corrupted circumcision by saying that the sign actually saves. There became an air of negligence with reference to the doctrine of baptism and there was no call for personal faith and repentance. So, what have we done to correct this? Unfortunately, we have thrown out the baby with the bathwater (literally)."

46 Time and space do not permit us to discuss the implications of familial solidarity, but if we could circumnavigate our twenty-first century, individualistic posture, and appreciate the communal posture of the people of God in the Scriptures, we would better understand why the New Testament mentions twelve household baptisms. We too quickly assume of these passages that they are pointing to "obvious, singular, individual conversions," but quite honestly, this might not have been the case. Perhaps households were baptized because the head of the household (and we *even* have a female example, Lydia (Acts 16), which should silence critique that the Bible is misogynistic and paternal—rather, it was way ahead of its time with reference to gender equality) believed, and the household was soon to follow suit. Moving towards maturity in the faith was a communal process—it was not achieved through an iPod and a flurry of self-help sermons. It was achieved through the sanctification of bumping up into family, friends, and church community, all sordid and imperfect, yet each working to bring about Christ-likeness in the other.

and each one should contain a certain number of seeds." You might choose to observe all of this advice. Or you might do only two or three of the five things that you were instructed to do. To the extent that you heed the advice will most likely be the measure to which your garden will grow to become healthy and sustainable. Yet, when it is all said and done, only God can make the garden grow.

Perhaps some of the ingredients that can lead to the "godward" life of a child are diligent discipline, fervent prayer, biblical instruction, proper peer selection, and appropriate involvement in the church's *means of grace* (baptism). God could use all of these to bring about his good pleasure in the life of your child. Yet, you might choose to administer only 2 or 3 of these practices. Perhaps this paper will cause you to consider adding a couple of ingredients to your parenting. However you choose to proceed, remember, it is only God who can sow the seeds of grace in your child's heart.

Finally, do not assume that the act of baptism will only be significant for your child if he or she is old enough to remember it. Rather, make this act special by celebrating it. Talk about the privilege of being baptized at such a tender age. As your family cycles through the calendar, celebrate it like you would a birthday or wedding anniversary. Have a special meal, complete with a favorite cake, and use the time to tell the story. Talk about the vow that you as a couple made to love and lead him in the way of Christ. Talk about the church body that also vowed to look after him and to love him as one of their own. Talk about how he stuck the microphone into his mouth or had a case of the hiccups. Talk about the minister's special prayer, and if you kept a copy of the worship folder, pull it back out and show it to him. May your child never have to know a day where he lived outside of the grace of God. To God be the glory for great things he has done![47]

---

[47] Richard Pratt. "Why Do We Baptize Our Children?" See *Third Millennium Ministries* (www.thirdmill.org) for information on acquiring this video. This video is one of the most concise resources on the subject and enabled me to write this booklet. When this booklet is lucid and helpful, it is indebted to Richard's work.